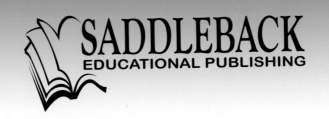

SADDLEBACK
EDUCATIONAL PUBLISHING

think green

Go Organic

ISBN-13: 978-1-59905-350-9
ISBN-10: 1-59905-350-0
eBook: 978-1-60291-678-4

Printed in Guangzhou, China
0812/CA21201151

16 15 14 13 12   3 4 5 6 7

Contents

Go Organic: An Introduction

The word *organic* refers to products that are manufactured using eco-friendly methods and materials. Organic products are natural and free from harmful pesticides, synthetic fertilizers, genetically modified organisms, antibiotics, and growth hormones. The reason to "go organic" comes from our knowledge that using or consuming organic products is good for our health, the health of our soil, the environment, and the planet.

Organic Agriculture

Organic agriculture promotes biological diversity and improves health quality for humans, soil, animals, and plants. It eliminates the use of artificial materials, chemicals, genetically engineered seeds, and pesticides. Organic crops grow in soil that has not been exposed to any kind of chemicals for at least three years. Organic agricultural techniques encourage the use of recyclable plant and animal waste. These wastes increase the nutrient level of soil, thereby enhancing and preserving its quality for future generations.

Organic Certification

All products sold as "organic" must be certified. Organic certification is a method of certifying food, other agricultural products, and livestock as organic. Certified organic food products must follow strict standards or guidelines at every step of production, processing, and packaging. The standards of organic certification vary in different countries. In the United States, the National Organic Program oversees the certification of all products sold as "organic."

History of Organic Farming

Organic farming is the oldest form of farming. However, during the first half of the 20th century, conventional farming became popular. Technological developments led to an increase in the use of pesticides, hormones, and synthetic fertilizers, as these chemicals helped increase agricultural production considerably. Although conventional farming was easier and more productive, widespread use of chemicals led to serious negative effects upon human health and the environment. After World War II, organic agriculture started to take root again. Lord Northbourne, in his book *Look to the Land*, which focused on healthy and eco-friendly methods of farming, coined the term "organic farming" for the first time in 1940.

Organic Livestock

Organic livestock is raised in a natural environment for meat, dairy products, and eggs. Farmers feed the livestock with 100% organic food and expose them to sufficient air, sunlight, and pasture. The animals are not given any kind of hormones and antibiotics to promote their growth.

Organic Labels

Organic labels indicate the percentage of organic ingredients in a product. Different products may have different labels, depending on their organic ingredients. Products that are purely organic are marked "100% Organic," while others may have different labels like "Organic," "Made with organic ingredients," or "Contains organic ingredients."

Did you know?

Earth loses one inch of topsoil every 28 years due to conventional farming. It takes nearly 3,000 years to build six inches of topsoil naturally, whereas organic farming can do the same in about 50 years.

Why Go Organic: Part 1

Going the organic way has many benefits for the environment and our health. By going organic, we ensure that we eat natural and healthy food. Organically produced foods are grown in organic soil, which nourishes and enriches the quality of the earth. By going organic, we make endurable use of Earth's resources. Going organic also prevents water and air pollution.

Health Benefits

- Organic food is free from toxic ingredients like herbicides, fungicides, and insecticides. According to the United States Environmental Protection Agency, about 60% of all herbicides, 90% of all fungicides, and 30% of all insecticides can cause cancer.
- Conventional farm workers are six times more vulnerable to health risks like cancer and pesticide poisoning than organic farm workers.

in the United States, while the remaining 99.5% is exposed to toxic chemicals. Switching to organic practices will help reduce the use of toxic chemicals and reduce pollution.

Organic Farming Benefits Wildlife

- The organic farming season starts in spring (as opposed to the conventional farming season, which starts in autumn) and allows weeds and other plants to grow on the land, which animals can feed on in the winter season.
- Organic livestock are not treated with antibiotics and deworming medicines. This helps dung beetles to survive as they live in animal waste. Dung beetles are a good source of food for many birds and help enrich the soil.
- Organic farmers maintain hedgerows that help birds build nests. Many birds are natural predators of harmful insects found in crops.
- Organic farmers do not remove weeds. Weeds are a source of food for many animals.
- Organic farming does not use pesticides. The use of pesticides in conventional farming has reduced the population of several species of animals. For example, the number of honeybees disappearing from the United States is dramatic. Honeybees are an essential pollinating agent for crops.

Organic Farming and the Food Chain

All plants and animals in an ecosystem are dependent on each other for their food. Conventional farming uses pesticides and fertilizers that can enter the food chain and harm consumers. Conventional farming also reduces the availability of food for many species, as only one particular crop is cultivated in a region. Organic farmers practice "mixed-crop farming," which means that different crops are cultivated in a region. Organic farming also practices crop rotation. This means that different crops are grown on the same land in successive years or seasons. Mixed-crop farming and crop rotation methods are good for the food chain and can feed diverse wildlife in a region.

Reduction of Toxicity and Pollution

Organic practices reduce the addition of toxic and poisonous substances to our environment. According to the United States Department of Agriculture (USDA), organic farming covers only 0.5% of agricultural land

Why Go Organic: Part 2

High Crop Yields

Scientists have found that organic farming practices can increase crop yields by almost 79%. For instance, organic farming increased maize yields by 20% to 250% in Brazil and by 150% in Peru. Even in drier climates and during droughts, organic farms produce higher yields than conventional farms.

Increase in Animal Reproduction

Studies show that animals reproduce better when fed with organic food. For example, chickens on an organic diet showed a 28% increase in egg production. Female rabbits produce two times more ova when fed with organic food.

Better for Future Generations

Consumption of conventional food has made our body a harmful chemical hub. By going organic, we can make our life and the life of future generations better.

Going Organic Saves Water

Groundwater is the most important source of drinking water. Groundwater in most places is contaminated with pesticides, nitrogen fertilizers, industrial chemicals, and heavy metals. Sediment runoff (animal manure and urine) from farmlands contaminates water in lakes and other water bodies. Organic farming helps reduce water pollution by avoiding pesticides and properly storing animal manure for composting.

Better for Biodiversity

- Organic farming encourages biodiversity and does not destroy natural landscapes.
- Mixed farming, an important aspect of organic farming, gives scope to raising livestock and crops together.
- Organic farming cultivates forage crops in rotation, which provides food for a wide range of animals.

- Organic soils have 1.6 times more invertebrate arthropods. This increases the availability of food for birds. Organic farms have 25% more birds than conventional farms.

Did you know?

Organic farms support twice as many butterflies as conventional farms.

Organic Farming

Organic farming is one of the fastest growing agricultural segments in the world. Most countries in the world are moving toward organically produced food to protect people's health and our planet. Although over the years conventional farming has produced food to feed the ever-increasing population of the world, it has also decreased soil fertility, converting acres of productive land into wasteland.

Organic Farming in the United States

The United States has seen tremendous growth in organic farming over the last decade. All 50 states have certified organic farms. The state of California has the maximum area of certified organic farmland. Other states with large areas of organic farmland include Alaska, Texas, and Montana.

Organic Farming in Australia

Australia has almost 29.6 million acres of organic farmland. It is one of the largest producers of organic products in the world. Australia exports almost 70% of its organic produce to Europe. Apart from organic fruits and vegetables, the Australian livestock industry is growing fast. Organic beef, sheep, and wool are in great demand.

Organic Farming in Argentina

Argentina is one of the top producers of organic products in the world. It exports about 80% of its organic produce. Argentina has about 6.9 million acres of organic farmland.

Organic Farming in China

China ranks third in organic farmland worldwide, after Australia and Argentina. It has about 5.7 million acres of organic farmland. China exports most of its organic products to nearby markets in Japan, Taiwan, and other Asian countries.

Organic Farming in Switzerland

Switzerland is one of the pioneers in organic farming. It has more than 6,300 organic farms. The Farmers' Movement started by Hans Müller and his wife Maria Müller in the 1940s initiated the organic-farming movement in Switzerland. They were the founders of organic farming in German-speaking countries. Hans Müller was the first in the world to use the term "organic-biological farming."

Organic Farming in the United Kingdom

Organic farming started in the United Kingdom in the 1930s. Lady Eve Balfour was one of the early pioneers of organic farming in the United Kingdom. According to the Department of Environment, Food, and Rural Affairs (DEFRA), the United Kingdom had about 1,704,964 acres of organic farmland in January 2005.

Benefits of Organic Farming

- Organic farming does not cause harmful chemicals to enter the food chain.
- Organic farming preserves natural areas like wetlands and fencerows that form an essential part of mixed farming.
- In conventional farming, the soil gradually loses its fertility due to use of artificial inputs. Organic farming methods enrich the soil with higher nutrients. Soil in organic farms is less acidic.
- Organic compost manure is an efficient soil builder. It increases the organic matter in soil and improves the quality of soil.

Organic Farming in Denmark

Denmark has one of the highest numbers of organic farms in the European Union. In 2002, there were about 3,714 organic farms, which accounted for about 6.7% of the total farmland. Organic farming has helped Denmark reduce its carbon dioxide emission significantly.

Organic Farming in Spain

Organic farming in Spain began in the 1970s. Spain has almost 3.5% of its farmland managed organically. At the end of 2006, it had around 17,214 organic farms, 1,942 organic processors, and 2,428 organic farms with animals.

Did you know?

Conventional farming uses about 350 different pesticides.

Organic Living

Organic living is a healthy way of life. It means eating food and using items that are pure and free from chemicals. It also means living in a toxin-free environment. By organic living, we can keep ourselves safe from the damaging effects of synthetic chemicals. Organic living is therefore beneficial for our health as well as the environment.

Organic Products

Buying organic products is one of the first steps to ensure an organic lifestyle. A wide range of products, both food and non-food items with different levels of organic ingredients, are available in stores and supermarkets. These products are toxin free and keep us safe from potential health problems.

Organic Clothing

Clothes made with conventionally produced fabric often have toxic ingredients. One of the most common fabrics used in clothes is cotton, which is one of the most pesticide-dependent crops. Clothes made from conventional cotton can therefore cause health problems. However, clothes made from organically grown cotton are free from any toxins. Chemical dyes used for coloring clothes are also harmful to human health. Organically grown colored cotton is a safer and cheaper alternative to dyes.

Did you know?

Sixty percent of what we apply on our skin is absorbed into our bodies.

Organic Skincare Products

The skin is the largest organ in the body and plays an important role in keeping us healthy. Everyday we use skincare products that are full of chemicals. Most of these chemicals are absorbed into the blood and can cause skin diseases such as eczema and allergies. Organic skincare products give the same results as chemical products but do not cause any adverse effects on our skin. Organic skincare products are chemical free because they are prepared using herbs and medicinal plants.

Organic Medicine

Organic medicines are prepared from organic plants. Most organic medicines have few or no side effects. In many countries, people use organic medicine to treat common illnesses. The term *organic medicine* is often used alternatively with *herbal* or *traditional medicines*. However, herbal or traditional medicines are not necessarily organic. They may use plants that have been grown conventionally.

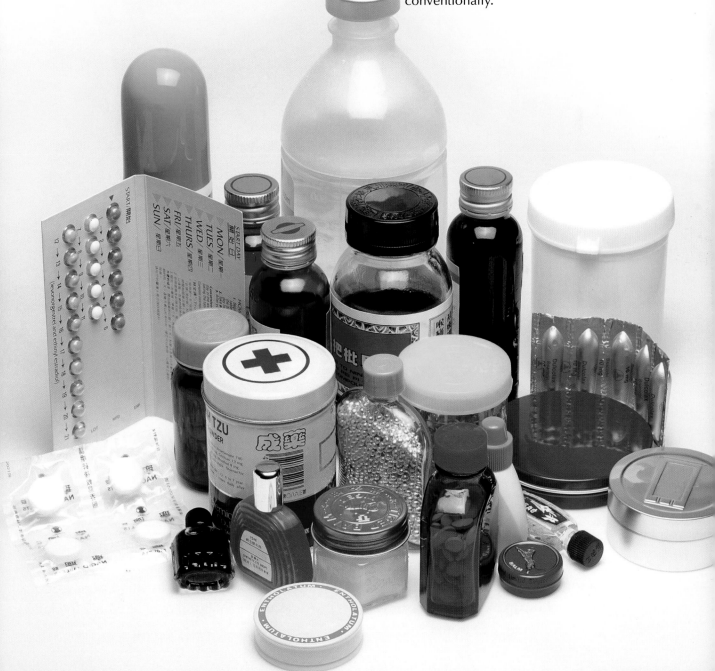

Organic Food

Organic food is grown in naturally enriched soil that has not been exposed to any chemical for a period of at least three years. Organic livestock is raised in a natural and healthy environment without being given any growth hormones. The animals are not confined to small pens but are allowed to roam about in large open pastures. This provides them a natural habitat where the land, vegetation, and water are free from toxins.

The Organic Food Industry

The organic food industry has been growing rapidly. The demand for organic food has reached an all-time high in recent years, as people become aware of the benefits. Organic food is grown in about 120 countries around the world. The European Union, Japan, and the United States are the global leaders in the organic food market. In the European Union, Germany is the leading consumer of organic food products, followed closely by the United Kingdom.

Organic Meat

Organic meat is a rich source of essential fatty acids and vitamin E. It is free of pesticide residues and is safer than any processed meat.

Organic Milk Is Healthier

Organic milk is a natural beverage. It is healthier than conventional milk because it contains 68% more omega-3 fatty acids. Omega-3 fatty acids are important nutrients that have a whole range of health benefits from improved cardiac, eye, and skin health to long-term memory retention. Organic milk is free from harmful antibiotics and growth hormones. It is also a rich source of calcium for growing children.

Organic Fish

Organic fish farming is done under natural conditions. Organic fish farms have enough space for fish to swim, and the fish are fed on high-quality recycled fish and shellfish waste. The fish are not treated with any kind of chemicals and are bred naturally without using hormones and antibiotics.

Did you know?

The global organic food industry is growing at the rate of 20% to 35% per year.

Better for Our Health

Organic fruits and vegetables are better for our health than any conventionally grown food. Most conventionally produced foods undergo massive refining that denatures them and removes their nutrients. Many harmful substances present in conventionally grown food can cause cancer, birth defects, and damage to body systems.

Cancer

Many cancer-causing chemicals such as vinyl chloride, arsenic, and benzene have been found in food items. Vinyl chloride, a chemical often used in food wrappings and containers, can cause severe damage to the liver cells if released into food. Similarly high levels of arsenic in food can cause skin and lung cancer. Many other fungicides and herbicides used in conventional farming are cancer-causing agents.

Nitrates in Food

Many conventionally grown foods, especially fruits and vegetables, have high concentrations of nitrates. Nitrates, when converted to nitrosamines, can cause cancer. They can also reduce the ability of blood to carry oxygen. Nitrate content in organically grown food is minimal, as fertilizers and chemicals are not used.

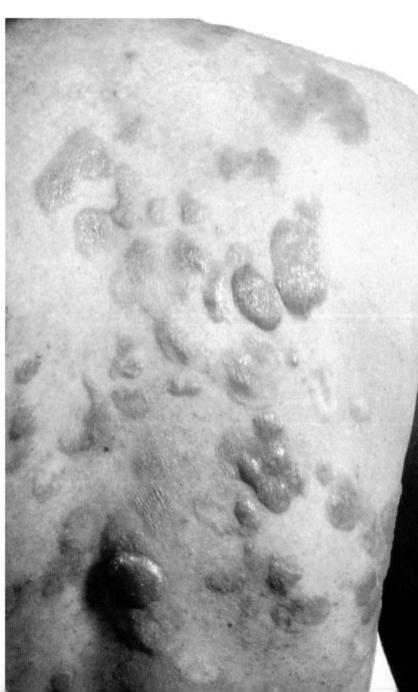

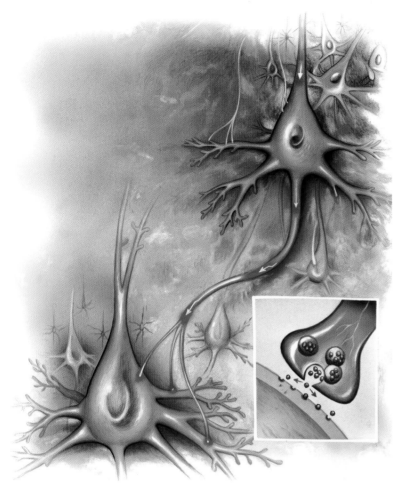

Hyperactivity

Many artificial colors and preservatives used in conventionally processed food and drink can cause hyperactivity in children. These colors and preservatives are not used in organic food items. Food additives have also been known to cause allergic reactions, headaches, asthma, and growth retardation in children.

Nervous System Disorders

Many chemicals in nonorganic produce are toxic to the brain, spinal cord, and other parts of the nervous system. These chemicals can cause muscle weakness, memory loss, and other severe damage to the nervous system.

Developmental Problems

Many harmful chemicals present in nonorganic food items have been found to cause birth defects. These chemicals can cause neurological disorders and suppress the development of the fetus.

Reproductive System Disorders

Conventionally grown and packaged foods often contain toxic chemicals that can damage the reproductive system in humans.

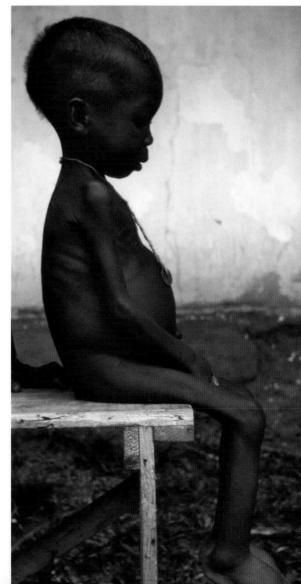

Nutritional Value

Organic food is nutritious. Most organic fruits and vegetables have considerably higher amounts of vitamins, minerals, enzymes, and micronutrients that are necessary to safeguard our health.

Healthy Living

- Organic food is healthy because no synthetic preservatives are added.
- Organic food is not genetically modified.
- Organic food helps relieve obesity.

Rich Source of Vitamins

Organic food contains higher levels of vitamin C than conventionally grown food. Organic fruits and vegetables have 27% more vitamin C, and frozen organic corn has 52% more.

Organic Soups and Salicylic Acid

Organic vegetable soup can supply more salicylic acid to the body. Salicylic acid has anti-inflammatory properties and cures body aches. It also prevents hardening of our arteries and bowel cancer. Salicylic acid is an important component of aspirin.

Antioxidants

Organically grown fruits and vegetables have higher levels of antioxidants. *Antioxidants* are chemical substances that protect us from diseases like cancer. Some antioxidants slow down aging in people and improve blood circulation. Studies have shown that organic strawberries and marionberries have almost 50% more antioxidants than conventionally grown strawberries and marionberries. Below is a list of organic fruits and vegetables that contain high levels of antioxidants:

Wild blueberry	Black plum
Broccoli raab	Blackberry
Cultivated blueberry	Red cabbage
Raspberry	Apple
Sweet cherry	Red kidney bean
Navel orange	Prune
Pinto bean	Pear (Red Anjou)
Red grape	Russet potato

Did you know?

Plants have about 5,000 to 10,000 natural compounds known as *phytonutrients*. They protect plants from pests and diseases.

Important Nutrients

Organic food contains:

- 21% more iron. Iron helps in hemoglobin formation. Hemoglobin is a part of the red blood cells that carry oxygen.
- 29% more magnesium. Magnesium reduces the rate of heart attacks and muscular contraction.
- 14% more phosphorus. Phosphorus helps in bone formation.
- 63% more calcium. Calcium is essential for stronger bones.
- 78% more chromium. Chromium deficiency can cause diabetes in adults and hardening of arteries.
- 70% more boron. Boron helps to prevent osteoporosis.
- 29% less lead. Lead adversely affects children's I.Q. (Intelligence Quotient).
- 25% less mercury. Mercury damages the nervous system.

The following table shows the average percentage difference of essential nutritional values of some common organic vegetables compared to conventional ones (the nutrition value of conventional food has been used as the baseline):

Vegetable	Vitamin C	Iron	Magnesium	Phosphorus
Organic Lettuce	+17%	+17%	+29%	+14%
Organic Spinach	+52%	+25%	-13%	+14%
Organic Carrot	-6%	+12%	+69%	+13%
Organic Potato	+22%	+21%	+5%	0%
Organic Cabbage	+43%	+41%	+40%	+22%

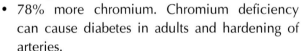

Chemicals in Conventional Food

Conventional foods contain many chemicals, additives, and contaminants. Vitamins and minerals are found naturally in food. They are essential nutrients that we need to stay healthy. Other chemicals called *additives* are added to conventional foods to enhance their taste, texture, color, and shelf life. Chemicals used while growing and manufacturing food may also remain in food as trace chemicals. These chemicals are called *contaminants*.

Food Additives

Food additives are materials used in food other than the raw ingredients. They are used to enhance color, flavor, aroma, or nutritional quality. Additives can be natural or synthetic. More than 90% of food additives are synthetic. Below is a list of food additives and diseases caused by using them in food:

- Tartrazine (102) is added in yellow- or orange-colored soft drinks. It can cause allergic reactions, headaches, asthma, growth retardation, and hyperactivity in children.
- Phosphoric acid is added as a sweetener in cola drinks. It can cause kidney-related problems and osteoporosis.
- Aspartame is the most commonly used synthetic sweetener. It is used in diet foods, chewing gum, fizzy drinks, breakfast cereals, frozen desserts, and yogurt. It can cause headaches, mood swings, vision problems, nausea, diarrhea, sleep disorders, and memory loss.
- Azorubine (Carmoisine) is a red-colored toxic chemical made from coal tar. It is used in the production of candy, gelatin crystals, puddings, cakes, jams, sauces, sweets, yogurt, and soups. It causes asthma and allergies. Azorubine is banned in Austria, Japan, Norway, Sweden, and the United States.
- Quinoline Yellow is a yellow, synthetic dye made from coal tar. It is used in the production of smoked fish, lipsticks, hair products, colognes, and in a wide range of medications. It may cause asthma, rashes, and hyperactivity. Quinoline Yellow is banned in Australia, Japan, the United States, and Norway.
- Yellow 2G (CI Food yellow 5 or Acid yellow 17) is a red-colored toxic chemical added in soft drinks. It is banned in Australia, Austria, Belgium, Denmark, France, Germany, Japan, Norway, Sweden, Switzerland, and the United States.

Contaminants

Traces of fertilizers or pesticides used in producing food can remain as contaminants. Pesticides found in conventional food include insecticides, miticides, and fungicides. Pesticides can cause serious short-term as well as long-term health problems.

Organophosphates

Organophosphates are a group of man-made chemicals. Organophosphates are the most widely used insecticides today. They are also one of the most harmful pesticides found in conventional food. Too much exposure to organophosphates can cause confusion, anxiety, loss of memory, loss of appetite, disorientation, depression, and personality changes.

Did you know?

Organic food contains 50% to 100% more minerals.

Protect the Newborn

Newborn babies and children are vulnerable to diseases. Babies have thin skin that absorbs chemicals and microbes very easily. Conventional baby items often contain chemicals and additives that can be dangerous to children. Using organic baby products can reduce this risk significantly. Organic baby products are safe and eco-friendly, which makes them suitable for babies.

Pesticides Are Harmful

Studies show that children are more prone to the effects of harmful pesticide residues than adults are. Children between the ages of two and four accumulate six times more pesticide residues in their bodies. This happens because their bodies are not fully developed to detoxify the toxic residues. Therefore, they have higher chances of being harmed by pesticide residues. This risk can be minimized by using organic products that do not have any of the harmful effects of pesticides on children.

Organic Baby Products

Organic baby products include:

1. Diapers
2. Bibs
3. Soaps
4. Shampoos
5. Lotions
6. Food products
7. Sponges
8. Oils
9. Crib mattresses
10. Blankets
11. Toys

Avoid These Fish

Eating certain predatory fish—those that eat other fish—is harmful for growing babies. Fish such as swordfish, shark, tilefish, king mackerel, and large tuna contain methylmercury, a chemical form of mercury, which is highly toxic. Children found eating these fish are known to suffer from neurological problems, which affect thinking ability, memory, language, and attention span.

Did you know?

A baby's digestive system digests more food and absorbs more nutrients, percentagewise, than an adult's. Along with nutrients, babies also absorb harmful pesticides. However, babies do not have fully developed kidneys. They are unable to excrete all harmful substances completely. These toxic substances remain in their bodies for a longer period and cause many disorders.

Crib Mattress

A baby spends most of her time on a crib mattress either sleeping or playing. This makes the crib mattress one of the most important products that a baby uses in her early life. Buying an organic crib mattress will keep your baby safe and healthy. Organic crib mattresses are natural and nontoxic and do not contain any chemicals or irritants. Crib mattresses use natural rubber, organic cotton, and wool. Rubber gives the best support to a baby's bone structure. Natural rubber used in organic crib mattresses is free from harmful chemicals, as it is extracted from rubber trees and not made from synthetic materials.

Baby Clothing

Organic cotton clothes are safer for newborns. Choosing organic clothing is the best way to protect the skin and health of babies.

Better for Our Planet

The world's population is growing at a rapid pace. There are more than six billion people living on our planet. This means that there is an ever-growing demand for more food. Most food is now produced through conventional methods, which is causing environmental problems like pollution and global warming. Adopting organic practices will reduce these problems.

Better for Soil

- Organic farming uses compost manure instead of chemical fertilizers. Compost manure is an efficient soil builder. Organic compost manure increases organic matter in soil and improves the quality of soil.
- Organic fields are better absorbers of water, too. Organic soil is more porous and allows water to percolate down to ground level quickly.
- Organic soil harbors useful bacteria. One teaspoon of organic soil can give shelter to 600 million to one billion helpful bacteria, whereas the same amount of chemically treated soil can host only around 100 helpful bacteria.

Organic Farming Is Energy Efficient

Conventional farming is highly mechanized and uses a lot of energy, whereas organic farming is labor intensive. In the United States, conventional farming uses about 12% of the total energy supply. Organic farming uses 30% less energy and water than conventional farming.

Organic farming does not use any artificial fertilizers. This reduces the amount of energy required by fertilizer industries and energy consumed in transportation. Organic products are generally grown, sold, and consumed locally. This practice also saves energy required in transportation.

Organic Farming and Global Warming

Most conventional farming practices emit greenhouse gases that contribute to global warming. However, organic soil reduces global warming by capturing carbon dioxide from the atmosphere and trapping it in the soil. Organic fertilizers used in organic farming help in trapping this carbon. An organic farm of 3.9 million cubic feet can trap about 1,000 pounds (about 0.5 ton) of carbon from escaping into the atmosphere.

Organic Farming Reduces Global Warming

- Organic farming uses compost, dairy waste, and cover crops that help increase organic matter or carbon in soil. Studies have shown that organic agriculture increases carbon in soil 15% to 28% over a period of 23 years. Carbon trapped in soil and vegetation is not easily released as carbon dioxide into the atmosphere.
- Organic farming doesn't use chemical fertilizers that emit nitrous oxide—a greenhouse gas.
- Organic farming does not use lime to make the soil suitable for farming. Adding lime to soil releases a lot of carbon dioxide into the air.
- Organic farming burns less fossil fuel to meet energy requirements. Conventional farmers, however, use fossil fuels extensively. This releases greenhouse gases, such as carbon dioxide, methane, and nitrous oxide, into the atmosphere.

Did you know?

In the United States, organic corn farms require about 30% less energy than conventional corn farms.

Food Standards

Food standards are guidelines approved by the government of respective countries for the production, handling, and processing of organic crops, livestock, and processed products. Organic food standards ensure the quality and safety of products. Food standards may vary with respect to different countries.

Organic Food Standards in the United States

- Use of conventional pesticides, chemical fertilizers, sewage sludge, and ionizing radiation are not permitted.
- Use of genetically modified seeds is prohibited.
- Organic livestock must be provided with 100% organic fodder.
- Use of antibiotics and growth hormones is restricted.
- Provide better information to consumers by affixing organic labels on food products so that consumers can understand the percentage of organic ingredients.

International Organic Food Standards: Codex Alimentarius Commission (CAC)

The Codex Alimentarius Commission is an international body formed under the initiatives of Food and Agriculture Organization (FAO) and World Health Organization (WHO) of the United Nations in 1963. It has 174 member countries. The objectives of the CAC are:

(a) to protect the health of consumers,
(b) to lay out international standards on food,
(c) to facilitate fair trading of food products, and
(d) to provide recommendations to the government of member countries to maintain food standards.

Did you know?

Ancient Egyptian, Chinese, Indian, Greek, and Roman literature also contains food regulations.

Similarities in EU and US Food Standards

Some of the similar organic food standards maintained by the European Union (EU) and the United States include:

- organic certification
- annual inspection of organic farms and products
- listing of ingredients on the side panel of the package
- a defined time to implement organic standards
- a well-developed farm plan, which would help increase production in future.

Differences in EU and US Food Standards

	United States	European Union
Crop conversion period	Requires a three-year conversion period with no exceptions	Requires two years for annuals and three years for perennial crops, with some exceptions
Manure restriction	Must be compost manure if applied within 120 days of harvest	Organic manure is generally preferred
Milk production	Certified as organic after 12 months on organic practice	Certified as organic after six months on organic practice
Organic livestock fodder	Requires 100% organic feed	30% to 60% of conventional feed is allowed
Organic labeling	Allows identification of organic ingredients on the information panel in products with 70% or less organic ingredients	Does not allow organic ingredients to appear on the label "Transition to organic" label is required in products produced during transition period

National Organic Standards Board

In the United States, an organic board was set up to develop national standards for all organic products. The board is called the National Organic Standards Board (NOSB). NOSB maintains regular communication with all organic communities in the United States to determine which substances used in production and processing will be allowed or prohibited. The NOSB also provides information and educates organic communities about the National Organic Program.

What is not allowed?

NOSB prohibits the use of irradiation, sewage sludge, or genetically modified organisms in organic production. The regulations also prohibit antibiotics and hormone use in organic meat and poultry. All organic livestock must eat a 100% organic diet.

Who is on the board?

The United States Department of Agriculture (USDA) appoints members to the National Organic Standards Board. The board has 15 members who serve five-year terms. The current board has four farmers, two handlers/processors, one retailer, one scientist, three consumer/public-interest advocates, three environmentalists, and a certifying agent.

NOSB Definition of "Organic"

The following definition of "organic" was passed by the NOSB at its April 1995 meeting in Orlando, Florida.

"Organic agriculture is an ecological production management system that promotes and enhances biodiversity, biological cycles, and soil biological activity. It is based on minimal use of off-farm inputs and on management practices that restore, maintain, and enhance ecological harmony.

" 'Organic' is a labeling term that denotes products produced under the authority of the Organic Foods Production Act. The principal guidelines for organic production are to use materials and practices that enhance the ecological balance of natural systems and that integrate the parts of the farming system into an ecological whole.

"Organic agriculture practices cannot ensure that products are completely free of residues; however, methods are used to minimize pollution from air, soil, and water.

"Organic food handlers, processors, and retailers adhere to standards that maintain the integrity of organic agricultural products. The primary goal of organic agriculture is to optimize the health and productivity of interdependent communities of soil life, plants, animals, and people."

NOSB and USDA

The NOSB serves as an advisory panel to the USDA. It recommends the use or prohibition of various substances in organic products. These recommendations later become a part of the rules that the organic industry follows. The NOSB forms technical advisory panels that evaluate all organic materials scientifically. It also advises the USDA on the effects of emergency pesticide spray programs in organic farms.

Did you know?

All recommendations made by the NOSB become official policy only when approved and adopted by the USDA.

Organic Labels

Organic labels confirm the organic status of food products. The labels also indicate the percentage of organic content in food products. The higher the percentage of organic content, the more eco-friendly the food product.

Organic Labels in the United States

The USDA certifies organic products in the United States. The products are classified into four categories, depending on the percentage of organic ingredients in them.

1. **100% Organic**
   Products with the "100% Organic" label are grown, handled, and processed using organic ingredients only.
2. **Organic**
   Products with the label "Organic" have at least 95% organic ingredients. The remaining 5% contain natural or synthetic ingredients that are not available in any organic form.
3. **Made from Organic**
   Products with the label "Made from Organic" contain 70% to 95% organic ingredients only.
4. **Less than 70%**
   The fourth category includes products that have less than 70% organic ingredients.

Organic Labels in France

In France, organic products are certified by Ecocert. Ecocert labels are approved by the French government. Ecocert uses the label "AB" for organic food products and the label "Cosmebio" for organic skincare products.

Organic Labels in Denmark

The Danish organic label is the Ø-mark. The mark is taken from the Danish word *Økologisk*, which means "organic." The label was launched in 1990. Imported organic goods sold in Denmark also carry this label. Many organic products also have the EU organic label along with the Danish label.

Organic Labels in the United Kingdom

In the United Kingdom, several organizations provide certification to organic products. The organizations have their own symbol and code number, and they are monitored by the Advisory Committee on Organic Standards (ACOS). The following organizations provide organic certification in the United Kingdom. Product packaging is labeled as follows:

1. UK1 UK Register of Organic Food Standards (UKROFS)
2. UK2 Organic Farmers and Growers Ltd. (OF&G)
3. UK3 Scottish Organic Producers Association (SOPA)
4. UK4 Organic Food Federation (OFF)
5. UK5 Soil Association Certification Ltd. (SA Cert)
6. UK6 Biodynamic Agriculture Association (BDAA)
7. UK7 Irish Organic Farmers and Growers Association (IOFGA)
8. UK9 Organic Trust Ltd.
9. UK10 CMi Certification
10. UK13 Quality Welsh Food Certification Ltd.
11. UK15 ASCISCO Ltd.

Organic Labels in Japan

In Japan, Japanese Agriculture Standard of Organic Agricultural Products (JAS) certifies organic products. All organic products from Japan have the JAS label on them.

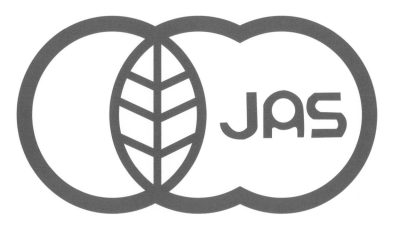

Organic Labels in Germany

In Germany, Bio-Siegel labels identify organic products. Bio-Siegel is the national eco-label of Germany.

Organic Labels in Switzerland

Bio Suisse is an association of Swiss organic agriculture organizations, which certifies most organic products in Switzerland. The organic symbol of Bio Suisse is a "bud."

Did you know?

The European Union (EU) has its own organic logo. This logo is used only on food products with at least 95% organic ingredients.

Organic Fibers

Organic fiber is natural fiber obtained from organically raised plants and animals. Unlike conventional fabric and textiles that depend on the use of strong chemicals and dyes, organic fiber is colored with eco-friendly dyes like clay. There are several kinds of organic fibers, such as cotton, wool, linen, hemp, etc.

Organic Cotton

Cotton is one of the most pesticide-dependent crops in the world. Organic cotton, however, is free from toxic chemicals, which can cause cancer, skin irritation, and other health problems. Organic cotton is softer than conventional cotton and is used to make clothing, home furnishings, and bedding.

Bamboo

Bamboo is a grass commonly used as a building material. Bamboo pulp fiber is used to make fabric. This fabric is naturally antibacterial, soft, and smooth. It can be worn in both summer and winter. It is one of the best fabrics for clothing, towels, and sheets.

Organic Wool

Organic wool fiber is obtained from sheep that are raised following organic standards. Organic sheep are not given any artificial growth hormones. They have ample exposure to sunlight and fresh air. Organic wool is softer, more durable, and more comfortable than conventional wool. Unlike conventional wool dyes that contain toxic heavy metals such as chrome, zinc, and copper, organic wool is colored using natural dyes. Organic wool is used to make blankets, knitting yarns, baby clothes, coats, socks, sweaters, and bedding materials.

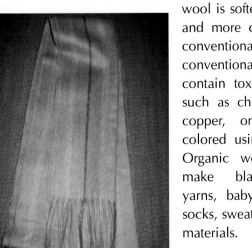

Conventional Cotton Is Dangerous

- Conventional cotton crops use 25% of the world's insecticides.
- Conventional cotton farming utilizes 10% of the world's pesticides including herbicides, insecticides, and defoliants.
- Conventional cotton products use almost 8,000 chemicals during production.
- Insecticides used in conventional cotton not only end up in the cotton, but in our air, water, and soil.
- Pesticides used in cotton farming cause almost 20,000 deaths every year in developing countries.

Organic Colored Cotton

Organic colored cotton is being developed to lessen the effects of harmful synthetic dyes that are used to prepare colored cotton fabrics. Natural colored cotton is less expensive than chemically dyed cotton. There are other advantages of naturally colored cotton, since it is friendly to sensitive skin and the color does not fade, even with repeated washing.

Hemp

Hemp is a natural fiber made from the hemp plant. Hemp cultivation does not require any pesticide, uses very little water, increases the quality of soil, and reduces erosion. Hemp fabric is completely biodegradable and is resistant to mold, bacteria, and chemicals. It is used to make all kinds of clothes, bags, hats, etc.

Did you know?

It takes almost 1/3 of a pound of chemicals (pesticides and fertilizers) to grow enough cotton for just one T-shirt.

Organic Silk

Silk is a natural fiber produced by silkworms. Organic silk is obtained from silkworms that are not treated with any pesticide or hormone. Clothes made with organic silk do not contain synthetic dyes. Organic silk is used to produce clothing, pillow batting, and bed linens.

Organic Clothing

Organic clothes are made from organic fibers. Cultivation of organic fibers consumes fewer resources and reduces the emission of carbon dioxide. Organic cotton, silk, bamboo, jute, wool, and hemp are common organic fibers.

Benefits of Organic Clothing

- Protects children
- Reduces pesticide use
- Protects farm workers
- Protects water quality
- Prevents soil erosion
- Provides sturdier fabric
- Soft and comfortable
- Saves money
- Reduces health risks
- Supports a true economy
- Supports a healthier environment

Organic Baby Clothing

Babies are particularly sensitive to chemicals. Babies' skin absorbs chemicals very easily. Therefore, infants and children should wear organic clothes, which do not contain any harmful chemicals.

Organic Bed Sheets and Pillowcases

Organic bed sheets and pillowcases are made using organic fibers such as organic cotton, hemp, silk, or bamboo fabric. They are free from harmful chemicals. Organic bed sheets and pillowcases are soft and smooth.

Organic Buckwheat and Millet Pillows

Buckwheat and millet crops are naturally resistant to insects. They are not dependent on pesticides and insecticides. Although buckwheat and millet are cultivated as food crops, they are also used to fill pillows. Buckwheat and millet pillows are eco-friendly and provide a healthy head support. They also provide relief from neck pain, headache, backache, and muscle pain.

Top Five Companies That Used the Most Organic Cotton in 2006:

- Wal-Mart (USA)
- Nike (USA)
- Coop Switzerland
- Patagonia (USA)
- Otto (Germany)

Did you know?

About 8,000 chemicals are used in the process of washing, bleaching, dyeing, and printing to make a T-shirt.

Avoid GM Food

Many agricultural crops such as rice, cotton, and maize have their genetic structure modified to achieve desired qualities. These crops are genetically modified. The process of altering genetic structure and creating a new organism is known as *genetic engineering*. For example, golden rice has been genetically modified to provide more vitamin A, which is good for eyesight. Other common GM foods are corn, soybeans, cottonseed oil, wheat, and canola oil.

Why are GM foods produced?

GM foods are produced to help farmers by reducing the cost and effort required to control insect pests, plant diseases, or weeds. GM foods can also meet the challenge to provide adequate food supplies for the rapidly increasing world population. Some advantages of GM foods:

- Pest resistant
- Herbicide tolerant
- Disease resistant
- Cold tolerant
- Drought tolerant/salinity tolerant
- Addition of extra nutrients in foods
- Genetically engineered plants clean heavy metal pollution from soil

What are genes?

Genes are a set of instructions found in the chromosomes of cells. Genes are the fundamental units of heredity and determine a particular trait in an organism. There are about 100,000 genes in the human body. Genes are transferred from parents to offspring.

Cloned Food

Cloned foods are milk or meat products produced from cloned cattle, goats, and pigs. Cloned foods are safe to eat, according to the United States Food and Drug Administration.

Harmful Effects of GM Food

1. **Damages Health** – Eating GM foods can hamper proper growth and cause diseases. A study conducted on rats showed that rats fed exclusively on GM foods did not grow properly. Ladybugs and lacewings, when fed on GM crops, were negatively affected. And 44% of monarch butterfly larvae died when fed milkweed dusted with pollen from GM corn, whereas caterpillars fed on normal corn pollen survived.

2. **Against Nature** – Genetic modification often mixes genes of different plants and animals to obtain the desired results. This method of producing new traits is against nature. For example, tomatoes are modified using a gene from a red fish to give them a bright red color.

3. **Allergic Reactions** – GM foods cause allergic reactions. Most food allergies are caused by specific proteins found in milk, wheat, fish, eggs, shellfish, peanuts, and soybeans. When proteins from these foods are incorporated into other food items during genetic modification, the modified foods may cause allergies in people.

Did you know?

Most of the world's genetic engineering is done in four countries: the United States (68%), Argentina (22%), Canada (6%), and China (3%).

Reduce Toxic Use

Toxins are poisonous substances that are harmful to humans, animals, and plants. They are present almost everywhere and pose a serious threat to our health and the environment. Every year about one thousand new chemicals enter the market. In the United States, about 80,000 different kinds of chemicals are presently being used.

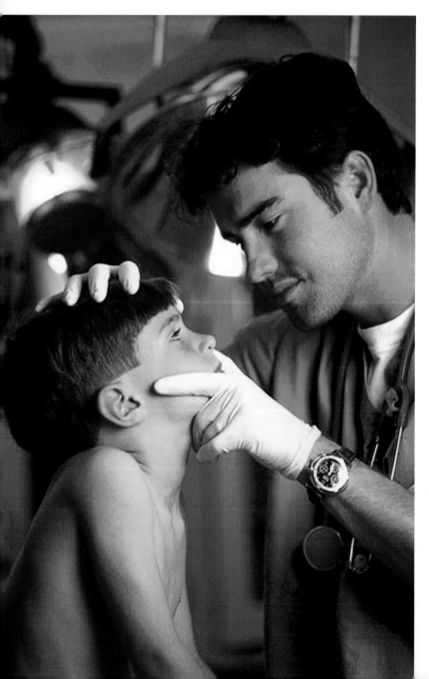

Health Disorders

Toxic chemicals can cause various problems in children and adults. Toxic effects can range from slight symptoms like headaches or nausea to severe symptoms like coma and even death. Children exposed to toxins can suffer from developmental and neurological disorders.

Reducing Toxic Substances in the Kitchen

- Do not use chemical air fresheners.
- Use organic products as much as you can.
- Do not use heavily scented products such as dishwashing liquids, washing powders, and floor cleaners.
- Use dishwasher detergents that are free from chlorine bleach and lower in phosphates (or phosphate free).
- Avoid canned food. Use fresh, frozen, or dried food.
- Use a water filter to reduce the chemical contaminants in drinking water.

Top Five Dangerous Chemicals at Home

- Cigarette smoke
- Lead
- Pesticides
- Formaldehyde
- Radon

Reducing Toxic Substances in the Bathroom

- Do not use cosmetics, toiletries, and perfumes with synthetic fragrances.
- Use soaps, shampoos, conditioners, and hair care products made of organic and natural ingredients.
- Use chlorine-free toilet paper.
- Use reusable, unbleached cotton towels, rags, and sponges.

Reducing Toxic Substances in the Garden

- Do not use pesticides, insecticides, herbicides, or any other chemical in the garden.
- Try to use natural and organic methods of gardening.
- Use paints, varnishes, and glues that are labeled as "Low VOC."
- Use less-toxic alternatives to chemical pesticides to control pests, such as insecticidal soap.
- Remove weeds by digging instead of using heavy toxic chemicals.

Did you know?

Cigarette smoke is a toxic pollutant that is made up of more than 4,000 chemicals.

Reducing Toxic Substances in the Living Room

- Do not use synthetic carpets, foam rubber, latex, or plastic coverings because these emit volatile organic compounds (VOC) that can cause cancer and developmental problems.
- Use carpets made of organic natural fibers such as wool, cotton, rattan, or jute.
- Remove shoes upon entering a home. Your shoes may have many harmful chemicals on them, such as pesticides, lead, and cadmium.

The Dirty Dozen

The "dirty dozen" is a list of the 12 most pesticide-contaminated fruits or vegetables consumed in the United States that are conventionally farmed. The list was compiled by the Environmental Working Group (EWG), a not-for-profit organization based in Washington, D.C. It is recommended that consumers purchase only organic versions of fruits and vegetables that are not members of the dirty dozen.

Environmental Working Group (EWG)

The Environmental Working Group is an environmental research organization. EWG works to improve public health and protect the environment by reducing air, water, and food pollution. EWG is made up of scientists, engineers, lawyers, policy experts, and computer programmers who study possible threats to human health and the environment. The dirty dozen list compiled by EWG has helped consumers become aware of the possible threats to their health.

EWG Tests

The original dirty dozen was based on the results of nearly 43,000 tests for pesticides on fruit and vegetable samples collected between 2000 and 2004. The latest edition of the dirty dozen is based on the results of nearly 51,000 tests for pesticides on fruit and vegetable samples collected between 2000 and 2005.

Dirty Dozen

According to the EWG, the dirty dozen are:

1. Peaches
2. Apples
3. Sweet bell peppers
4. Celery
5. Nectarines
6. Strawberries
7. Cherries
8. Lettuce
9. Grapes (imported)
10. Pears
11. Spinach
12. Potatoes

Did you know?

In the United States, consumption of pesticides increased by 70 million pounds between 1996 and 2003.

Multiple Combinations of Pesticides

Fruits with the most pesticide combinations overall were apples, followed by peaches and strawberries. Apples had a combination of up to 50 pesticides, followed by peaches with 42 pesticides and strawberries with 38 pesticides.

Most Pesticides

Fruit is the most contaminated food in the list, with seven of the 12 items being fruit. Among the top six are four fruits, with peaches topping the list. Nectarines have the highest percentage of samples that tested positive for pesticides.

Multiple Pesticides

Peaches had the most likelihood of multiple pesticides on a single sample, followed by nectarines and apples. The most multiple pesticides were found in peaches and apples followed by strawberries. Eating these fruits and vegetables will make a person vulnerable to about 14 pesticides per day.

The Clean Dozen

The "clean dozen" is a list of the 12 least pesticide-contaminated fruits or vegetables compiled by the EWG that are conventionally farmed. The clean dozen list was based on the results of nearly 43,000 pesticides tests on fruits or vegetables. Consumers who are on tight budgets may purchase conventionally farmed fruits and vegetables that are members of the clean dozen.

Avoiding Pesticides

People can lower their exposure to harmful pesticides by eating clean dozen fruits and vegetables. This can reduce pesticide risk by almost 90%. Eating clean dozen fruits and vegetables will only expose a person to less than two pesticides per day.

Few Pesticides

Fruits and vegetables on this list have very few pesticides. The highest number of pesticides found on the clean dozen list was four. Nearly three-quarters of vegetables like eggplant, broccoli, and cabbage had no detectable pesticides in them.

Did you know?

Pesticides from fruits and vegetables can be reduced by peeling or washing them properly.

The Clean Dozen Are:

1. Onions
2. Avocados
3. Sweet corn (frozen)
4. Pineapples
5. Mangoes
6. Sweet peas (frozen)
7. Asparagus
8. Kiwis
9. Bananas
10. Cabbage
11. Broccoli
12. Eggplant

Cleanest Five

Vegetables are the cleanest food. The cleanest five of the clean dozen list are fruits and vegetables that are least likely to have pesticide residues on them. Pesticide residues are pesticides that remain in food after they are applied to food crops. The cleanest five are onions, avocados, sweet corn (frozen), pineapples, mangoes, and sweet peas (frozen).

The Fallen Fruit Project

The Fallen Fruit Project is a program that encourages mapping and sharing of fruit grown in public places. The program was started by three Los Angeles artists who believed that cities are full of trees, shrubs, and bushes that merely add to the beauty of the place. The Fallen Fruit Project promotes the planting of fruit trees, which would bear fruit for all, provide shade, and at the same time look beautiful too. If they are grown organically, then it helps the environment also.

Objectives of the Fallen Fruit Project

- To map all public fruit trees in a neighborhood.
- To request that property owners plant fruit trees on the periphery of their property so that all can share the fruit.
- To ask municipal authorities to plant fruit trees in parks, parking places, and on street sides.
- To make municipal authorities aware that all plants should be grown organically and conventional methods should be avoided.
- To encourage urban planning authorities to replace ornamental trees with fruit trees.

Public Fruit Park Project

The Public Fruit Park Project aims to have fruit parks on unused land in urban areas. The objectives of the project are:

- To plant fruit trees such as avocados, loquats, persimmons, pomegranates, figs, walnuts, and guavas, as they need little care and less water.
- To protect local native fruit trees.
- To involve the local community in taking care of the park.
- To protect the environment by growing fruits organically.
- To share the fruit with all visitors to the park.

Nighttime Fruit Forages

Nighttime fruit forages are fruit walk events conducted at night. Activists of the Fallen Fruit Project walk through a neighborhood with new members carrying picking bags and flashlights to pick fallen fruit. Nighttime fruit forages last from 60 to 90 minutes.

Endless Orchard

Endless Orchard is a proposal to convert 17 acres of public green space in Los Angeles into an endless orchard. The orchard will be designed in rows of 10 by 10. Three sides of the orchard will be enclosed with mirrored walls, and there will be sinks outside the walls to wash fruit. The orchard will be full of fruit trees like plums, peaches, apricots, nectarines, and pluots. Fruit will be available throughout the year, as all fruit trees planted will have different ripening seasons.

Public Fruit Jam

Public Fruit Jam is a community jam-making session arranged by the Fallen Fruit Project in Los Angeles, California. Participants bring in homegrown or public fruit and empty canning jars and take part in the jam-making session. Everyone gets a share of the jam, even those who come empty-handed.

Did you know?

Green waste fills one-third of household garbage cans.

Organic Food Myths

As the popularity of organic food increases, several myths have been created. These myths create confusion in the minds of people about organic food. These myths can strongly influence people's beliefs.

Myth: Organic food means only fresh fruits and vegetables.
Truth: Organic food products can be anything from food to beverages.

Myth: There is no way of knowing if something is organic.
Truth: Consumers can rely on certification when buying organic. Certified organic labels are the best way to verify an organic food product. Most countries have their own standards of certification of organic products.

Myth: Organic farming is unkind to animals.
Truth: Animal welfare is one of the most important principles of organic farming. Animals are provided proper diet and handled with a lot of care.

Myth: Organic farming uses pesticides that damage the environment.
Truth: Organic farming methods are free from synthetic fertilizers, pesticides, and herbicides. Organic farming relies on chemical-free methods of farming.

Myth: Everything in a natural food store is organic.
Truth: Natural food stores sell not only organic food but also conventional food products. Buying a food product from a natural food store does not mean that it is organic.

Myth: Organic foods are no healthier than nonorganic foods.
Truth: Organic food contains fewer contaminants. Studies have shown that organic food has more nutrients than conventional food.

Did you know?

Plant-based organic foods have about 25% more fiber than their nonorganic counterparts.

Control Farm Pollution

Farm pollution is a serious threat to human life and the environment. Farm pollution is caused by farm waste that pollutes rivers and contaminates groundwater. Common farm waste includes organic manure, animal carcasses, slurry, pesticides, crop residue and debris, and sewage sludge.

Did you know?

In the United States, about 24 million pounds of antibiotics are used to speed up livestock growth.

Dangerous Pesticides

Conventional farming uses various pesticides in a single growing season. Farmers often tend to use too much and too many pesticides. Although these pesticides help control unwanted plants, pests, and diseases in crops, it also leaves harmful residues in the soil. Excessive use of pesticides contaminates groundwater and fresh water supplies in a region. This causes air and water pollution, which leads to many health problems in humans and animals.

Deadly Pits and Carcasses

Animals generate 130 times more waste than humans do. Animal manure in farms is stored in manure pits. These manure pits contaminate groundwater and pollute nearby water bodies like lakes and rivers. Manure pits also generate deadly gases that cause nausea, skin infections, and respiratory problems. Animal manure contains phosphorous and ammonia which are beneficial for plants but are very harmful for aquatic ecosystems. Ammonia kills fish and other aquatic life. Carcasses of dead livestock are another source of farm pollution. Carcasses should be cremated within 24 hours or buried away from any drinking water supply, waterway, or field drain.

Slurry

Slurry is animal manure mixed with water. Many farms use slurry as liquid fertilizer. Slurry can pollute rivers, streams, and lakes if applied incorrectly. Excess nutrients that are not absorbed by plants and soil seep into the ground and contaminate groundwater. Slurry decreases oxygen levels in water bodies, causing fish to suffocate and die.

Irrigation

Irrigation helps in the proper growth of crops. However, excessive irrigation accumulates pesticides and other nutrients, which reduces soil fertility. Farmers can control pollution from irrigation by efficiently using irrigation water.

Health Problems Caused by Pesticides

- Nausea
- Muscular weakness
- Irritation of eye, nose, and throat
- Central nervous system disorders
- Increased risk of cancer
- Damage to liver and kidneys

Go for Biodiversity

Biodiversity means the variety of lifeforms living in a region or environment. This includes plants, animals, and their diverse species. Biodiversity is the natural result of evolution and allows ecosystems to function properly. The interactions among these diverse plants and animals form the food chain and the complex web of life. The Earth's biodiversity is now in danger because of shrinking forests, spreading deserts, polluted air and water, and rising temperatures.

Types of Biodiversity

There are three main types of biodiversity:

1. *Genetic diversity* includes genetic differences between individuals or groups of individuals in a specific species. For example, differences among breeds of dogs, ethnicity of humans, and varieties of plants. These differences are a result of genes found in the cells of organisms.
2. *Species diversity* includes diversity among various plant and animal species. For example, the diverse plant kingdom includes more than 250,000 species of plants, while there are more than one million species of insects.
3. *Ecosystem diversity* is the variety of habitats and includes deserts, forests, wetlands, mountains, lakes, rivers, and agricultural landscapes.

Benefits of Biodiversity

The entire ecosystem works under biodiversity. The benefits and services provided by ecosystems include:

1. **Generation of Soil and Maintenance of Soil Quality**

   Soil contains numerous living organisms like bacteria, algae, fungi, mites, and worms. These living organisms help in the decomposition of organic matter. Decomposition of living organisms in the soil releases essential nutrients like nitrogen, carbon, and phosphorous, all of which benefit plants.

2. **Maintains Air Quality**

   Plants play a vital role in the purification of air. They convert carbon dioxide into oxygen and improve air quality.

3. **Maintains Water Quality**

   Living organisms of wetland ecosystems recycle nutrients and sewage. Forests improve soil quality and reduce soil erosion and landslides.

4. **Pest Control**

   Natural pest controllers like insects, birds, and fungi work better than artificial pesticides. These natural pesticides reduce the possibility of air, water, and soil contamination.

5. **Detoxification and Decomposition of Waste**

   Decomposing organisms present in the soil help in decomposing all industrial, commercial, and agricultural waste. This decomposed waste provides essential nutrients to plants.

6. **Pollination and Crop Production**

   Animals help in pollination and crop production. About one-third of crops are the result of natural pollination. Bees, butterflies, bats, birds, etc. are natural transporters of pollen.

Did you know?

India has the world's two most important biodiversity centers, located in the Western Ghats and in the Eastern Himalayas.

Threats to Biodiversity

Many factors threaten the biodiversity on Earth. The major threat, however, is from human activity. Some of these factors are:

- Rapidly growing population increases the demand for food. This leads to deforestation, which affects the diversity of plant and animal species.
- Over-hunting and over-fishing for commercial use have also reduced the population of various fish and animals.
- A rapidly growing population also demands shelter. In the United States, between 1992 and 1997, around 16 million acres of forest, cropland, and open space was converted into residential areas.
- Global climate changes affect the habitat of many animals. The population of penguins has shrunk by 33% in the last 25 years. Studies have revealed that around 60% of Northern Hemisphere habitats will be affected by global warming.
- About 300,000 species of animals have become endangered or extinct in the last 50 years due to illegal trade and hunting.
- Use of chemical pesticides affects insect pollination.
- Use of chemical pesticides also contaminates the air and water and causes acid rain. Acid rain causes damage to animals, plants, lakes, forests, buildings, and monuments.

Organic Cleaning Products

Organic cleaning products are usually made up of plant-based ingredients and essential oils. They are safe and eco-friendly and do not contain perfumes or dyes. Organic cleaning products such as dish detergent, soaps, and cleaners usually contain herbal antibacterial substances that are safe for human health and the environment.

Avoid Nonorganic Cleaning Products

Nonorganic cleaning products contain harmful toxins such as neurotoxins, irritants, and heavy metals that can cause cancer, respiratory problems, and behavioral problems. Nonorganic cleaning products can also contribute to ozone layer depletion, pollute groundwater, contaminate soil, and harm plant and animal life.

Organic Cleaning Products Are Better

Organic cleaning products are better because they are derived from vegetables, are nontoxic and non-hazardous, and are free from phosphates, chlorine, petrochemicals, and genetically modified organisms. They are also biodegradable.

Vinegar

Vinegar is an organic cleaning product that can be used both as a disinfectant and as an air freshener. It is useful for cleaning mineral deposits on glass, appliances, the stovetop, floors, and other smooth surfaces. It can also be used as a natural fabric softener. Vinegar can be used for killing most mold, bacteria, and germs.

Baking Soda

Baking soda is a natural substance used for cleaning. It can be used to scrub surfaces and clean and polish metals. Baking soda works as a great deodorizer, too. It is used as a fabric softener and dishwashing detergent.

Natural Cleaning Ingredients

- Cornstarch
- Baking soda
- Mineral oil
- Borax
- White chalk
- Salt
- Talcum powder

Lemon Juice

Lemon juice works well as an all-purpose cleaner. It can be used to remove stains and clean glass, brass, and copper. Lemon juice can be used to scrub dishes and surfaces. It also acts as a natural bleaching agent and as an antiseptic.

Environmentally Friendly Furniture

Environmentally friendly furniture is made from the wood of fast-growing trees like mango or grasses like bamboo. Such furniture spares the wood of threatened species like teak and mahogany. Environmentally friendly furniture is not polished or varnished with chemicals. Conventional furniture contains chemicals like formaldehyde, which causes wheezing, nausea, skin irritation, and cancer.

Use of Recycled Materials

Environmentally friendly furniture makers often use recycled materials to create new and useful furniture. This helps reduce landfill space and lessens the demand for energy. Floorboards, wood siding, pallets, and railroad ties are often recycled to make furniture.

Environmentally Friendly Strawboard Panels

Strawboard panels are made from raw wheat or rice straw. Strawboard panels are used to make frame structures, partitions, flooring, ceilings, and roofs. They can replace the use of interior drywall. Strawboard panels are environmentally friendly, economical, and can be recycled. They are durable, fire proof, and termite resistant. According to the National Resource Defense Council, recycling straw eliminates the problem of disposing of 140 million tons of straw annually and saves one acre of forest.

Organic Furniture

Organic furniture is made from certified organic and chemical-free wood. The production of this furniture reduces pollution and does not cause any health problems. Production is in harmony with space, environment, and health.

Eco-Friendly Cardboard

Furniture made from cardboard is eco-friendly, lightweight, portable, inexpensive, and recyclable. Cardboard furniture can replace many of our conventional furniture pieces without cutting down new trees.

Why use environmentally friendly furniture?

- Environmentally friendly furniture is free from harmful chemicals and dyes and therefore nontoxic.
- Most environmentally friendly furniture is recyclable.
- Some environmentally friendly furniture can be easily assembled.
- Environmentally friendly furniture does not use paints and polishes that contain harmful chemicals.

Tips to Buying Environmentally Friendly Furniture

- Buy furniture made from recycled materials.
- Buy furniture made from bamboo.
- Buy furniture made from recycled metal or plastic.
- Buy ready-to-assemble and recyclable furniture.
- Buy fixable and durable furniture.
- Buy low-toxic furniture.

Did you know?

Every year, American consumers buy about three million desks, 16.5 million chairs, 4.5 million tables, and 11 million file cabinets. About half of this amount is disposed of annually.

Organic Gardening

Organic gardening uses natural methods to grow vegetables and fruit. Most maintenance work on an organic garden is done manually. Vegetables and fruit are grown using natural manure. All pesticides used to control diseases, insects, and weeds in organic gardens are natural.

Why organic gardening?

- Compost can easily be prepared by recycling garden and kitchen waste.
- Fruits and vegetables are not genetically modified and are free from pesticides, plus the gardening methods are environmentally friendly.
- Saves money as expensive chemicals are not used
- Reduces soil and water pollution and prevents soil erosion
- Organically grown food is more nutritious and healthful.
- Reduces exposure to chemicals and synthetic fertilizers
- Helps biodiversity and protects heirloom plants

How to Make Your Own Organic Garden

- Decide what you want to grow according to the available space.
- Use natural compost to improve the quality of the soil.
- Add organic matter to the soil regularly.
- Make your own compost by recycling vegetable and plant scraps.
- Grow vegetables and plants that are disease and pest resistant. Use organic methods to control pests, such as companion plants that naturally repel unfriendly insects.
- Do not grow the same type of plants in a large area. Grow plant companions. Try to grow scented flowers next to edible crops.
- Inspect your garden regularly. Prevent growth of weeds using various types of mulch. Pull weeds manually as needed.

How to Make Your Own Compost

Compost can be made by adding fallen leaves, straw, dead flowers, shredded newspaper, grass clippings, vegetable peelings, fruit rinds, eggshells, and barnyard animal manure. Avoid meat, dairy, and cooked food, as they can attract vermin.

Some Combinations for Companion Planting

- Roses with chives
- Tomatoes with cabbage
- Cucumbers with nasturtiums
- Peppers with pigweed or ragweed
- Corn with beans
- Lettuce with tall flowers
- Radishes with spinach
- Potatoes with sweet alyssum
- Cauliflower with dwarf zinnias
- Collards with catnip
- Strawberries with love-in-a-mist

Did you know?

In the United Kingdom, kitchen waste amounts to about 21% of the total waste produced annually.

Companion Planting

Companion planting is a technique of growing plants in combination. Growing two different species of plants together improves soil fertility. Companion planting also helps control pests. Companion planting uses garden space efficiently and makes the garden look beautiful too. For example, one can grow French marigolds in combination with tomatoes. A strong odor released from marigolds will keep green and black flies away from tomatoes.

Organic Fertilizers

Organic fertilizers are natural fertilizers made from plant and animal residues or their by-products. Some organic fertilizers are manufactured, while others occur naturally. Compost, blood meal, bone meal, and seaweed extracts are manufactured organic fertilizers. Limestone, mine rock phosphate, and sulfate of potash are naturally occurring minerals used as organic fertilizers.

Some Organic Fertilizers Are:

- Seaweed
- Fish emulsion
- Humates
- Molasses
- Bone meal
- Corn gluten meal
- Greensand
- Lava sand
- Epsom salt
- Compost
- Mulch
- Worm castings
- Chicken or bat manure
- Gypsum
- Hydrogen peroxide
- Lime

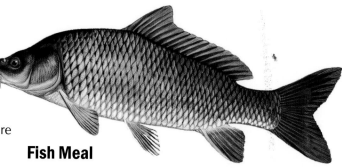

Fish Meal

Fish meal is a protein-rich organic fertilizer. It is dried fish in its ground form. Fish meal is usually made from oil-rich small fish like menhaden or anchovy. It is rich in phosphorus and nitrogen, which makes it an excellent food for plants.

Manure

Manure comes from animal excretion. It is rich in nutrients and is used as a fertilizer to enrich soil.

Seaweed

Seaweeds are saltwater plants. Seaweeds such as algae, bladder wrack, and kelp are good organic fertilizers. Seaweeds help stimulate root growth in plants.

Blood Meal

Blood meal is a nitrogen-rich organic fertilizer made from dried and powdered animal blood. It is used as a liquid fertilizer by mixing it with water.

Peat

Peat is partially decomposed plant matter that is used as an organic fertilizer. Peat is generally formed in swamps, wetlands, and bogs.

Worm Castings

Worm castings are worm manure. These are undigested materials or bacteria excreted by worms. The castings contain plant nutrients and growth-enhancing compounds. Earthworm castings increase soil fertility and quality.

Benefits of Adding Organic Matter to Soil

- Improves soil quality by providing enough exposure to air and temperature
- Harmless to organisms living in the soil
- Strengthens soil to hold water and other nutrients
- Dissolves minerals into soil to improve soil quality
- Reduces waste landfills by recycling organic waste

Benefits of Organic Fertilizers

Organic fertilizers do not contain synthetic chemicals and therefore cause less pollution. They are good for humans, animals, and the environment.

- Organic fertilizers ensure that food grown by organic farming is free of harmful chemicals.
- Organic fertilizers cost less than synthetic fertilizers.
- Organic fertilizers can be prepared easily at the farm.
- Use of organic fertilizer enriches nutrient content of soil and reduces the amount of fertilizer required every year. Synthetic fertilizers reduce soil fertility.
- Organic fertilizers do not contaminate land and water.

Did you know?

The United States consumes 21 million tons of fertilizers annually.

Vermicompost

Vermicompost is a kind of organic compost made by worms. Some species of earthworms, like red earthworms, break up organic waste such as food scraps, paper, and plants to form compost. This process of breaking down organic waste is known as *vermicomposting*. Bacteria and earthworms are important agents of vermicomposting.

Benefits of Vermicompost

- Vermicomposting produces organic fertilizer, which is safe for the environment.
- Vermicomposting is a cost-effective process.
- The levels of nutrients like nitrogen, phosphorous, and potassium in vermicompost are five to 11 times more than synthetic fertilizers.
- Vermicomposting takes less than two months to produce rich worm compost.
- Worms also destroy bacteria like *E. coli*, viruses like salmonella, and parasitic worm eggs.
- Vermicomposting helps in recycling organic matter into the soil and crops.

How to Make Vermicompost

- Place a polythene sheet at the bottom of the worm bin.
- Add 5–7 inches of organic waste.
- Use shredded newspaper, corrugated cardboard, coarse sawdust, dry leaves, or seaweed to make the bedding for worms.
- Add a layer of cow manure slurry on top of the waste.
- Leave the waste to decompose for 20 days.
- Put worms in the bin to start casting.
- Cover the bin properly to keep fruit flies and birds out.
- Water the bin every 3 days for 2 months to maintain the moisture in the bin.
- Separate the worms from compost after 2 months.
- Use these worms for making future vermicompost.

Dos and Don'ts of Vermicomposting

- Feed worms at equal intervals.
- Add more food scraps as their population grows.
- Bury the waste under the soil to avoid fruit flies and odors.
- Bad smells indicate that you are putting in more than enough food. Avoid doing so.
- Do not put plastic bags, bottle caps, rubber bands, sponges, aluminum foil, or glass in the vermicomposting bins. They are harmful for worms.
- Avoid using insecticides near the worm bin.
- Keep the worm bin in a shaded area away from direct sunlight or heavy rain.

Waste Menu for Worms

Worms in the worm bin can be fed with all kitchen and garden waste. Worms love eating vegetable and fruit scraps. They can also be given soaked and ripped pizza boxes, shredded and soaked cardboard, paper, leaves, tea bags, and eggshells. Worms, however, do not like to eat onions and citrus fruit because of their oil content and strong smell.

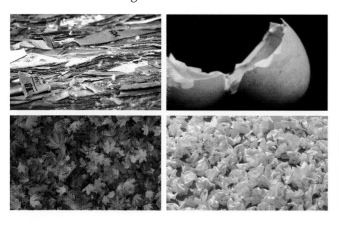

Benefits of Vermicomposting

- Helps in plant growth and increases crop yield
- Increases crop quality and taste
- Reduces soil erosion
- Reduces the amount of salt and acid in soil
- Improves soil productivity
- Improves plant resistance to pests and diseases
- Controls pollution

Did you know?

Red worms can live up to 4½ years in a composting bin, while in the wild they live up to one year.

Make Your Own Organic Bread and Coffee

Bread is made from grain flour. The most common grain used to make bread is wheat. Coffee is a common beverage made from roasted and ground coffee beans. The coffee plant is a shrub or small tree native to subtropical Africa and southern Asia.

Why eat organic bread?

- Easier to digest
- Rich in nutrients
- Reduces cholesterol
- Free from preservatives and additives
- Best for people who cannot digest milk and milk products

Organic Bread

Organic bread is made from organic food materials. The flour used in organic bread is grown organically. Special care is taken in the process, from kneading to baking of the bread. Organic bread is prepared without using any artificial preservatives or color.

Make Your Own Organic Bread

Ingredients required for the whole-grain loaf recipe:
- Whole-grain organic flour
- Mixed dried fruit
- Tea
- Fresh organic yeast
- Organic sugar
- Melted organic butter
- Warm organic milk
- Salt
- Mixed spices

Instructions

1. Put 1 cup mixed dried fruit in a bowl, cover with 1¼ cups of tea, and leave it overnight.
2. Pour ⅔ cup of milk into a saucepan and heat the milk. Pour the warm milk into a medium bowl. Add ¼ cup of sugar and 2 tablespoons of fresh yeast into the warm milk. Leave the mixture for 15 to 20 minutes.
3. Put 1 pound whole-grain flour in a mixing bowl. Add 1 teaspoon of salt, 1 teaspoon of mixed spices, and the mixed dry fruit. Melt ¼ cup of butter and add to the mixture. Mix it well.
4. Add a little water if necessary, and knead the dough for 5 minutes. Allow the dough to rise for 1½ hours.
5. Knead the dough again and fit it into a greased baking pan.
6. Let it sit for another 25 minutes.
7. Bake the bread in an oven preheated to 400° F for 35 minutes.

Who produces the most organic coffee?

The leading producers of organic coffee in the world are Mexico, Costa Rica, Guatemala, Nicaragua, and Peru.

Organic Coffee

Organic coffee is grown in the shade using traditional means only. In the production of organic coffee, only organic pesticides and fertilizers are used. Organic coffee is grown in more than 30 countries across the world, including the United States.

Did you know?

Latin America and East Africa produce 70% of the world's organic Arabica coffee.

Make Your Own Organic Coffee

Ingredients:
- ¼ cup of organic espresso
- 2 tablespoons of organic chocolate syrup
- ½ cup of organic milk
- Dollop of organic whipped cream

Instructions

- Keep your chocolate syrup at room temperature.
- Prepare ¼ cup espresso.
- Steam the organic milk.
- Keep the tip of the steam wand just below the surface for more foam, or submerge the wand farther into the milk for less foam.
- Pour the syrup into a mug; add espresso and then the hot milk.
- Top with a dollop of organic whipped cream.

Why drink organic coffee?

- Buying organic coffee helps organic farmers economically.
- Natural methods used in organic coffee production are healthier for the farmers.
- Organic coffee does not use chemicals and therefore prevents water, soil, and air pollution.

Index

Glossary

acid rain: rain that has become acidic due to airborne pollutants

acidic: water or soil having a pH level less than seven

algae: rootless plant such as seaweed

aquatic: ability to live or grow in or on water

bacteria: single-celled organisms that can cause disease

biodegradable: substance that can be broken down naturally and harmlessly

biodiversity: variety of living organisms present in a given habitat

bleach: to remove color from a substance

component: part that combines with other parts to make up a whole

contaminant: a substance that can cause adverse effects on air, water, or soil

decompose: to break down and decay

decomposition: process in which organic materials are broken down

deforestation: removal of forests

dissolve: to break up into particles in a liquid

drought: a period of time without any rain

ecosystem: a complex community of living things in a physical environment

emission: substance discharged into the air

endangered: in danger of dying out or becoming extinct

environmentalist: a person who works to protect the environment from destruction or pollution

erosion: wearing away of land or soil by water, wind, animals, and even human activity

extinct: a species that is no longer living or existing

fertilizer: chemical substance used to improve soil and promote plant growth

fossil fuel: fuel derived from organic remains, such as petroleum, coal, and natural gas

founder: person who establishes a group or community

global warming: increase in the average temperature of the Earth

habitat: an environment in which a plant or animal normally lives and grows

heavy metals: metals that are harmful to human health, such as mercury and lead

hemisphere: half of the Earth on either side of the equator

herb: plant grown for medicinal or aromatic purposes, such as fern or wild ginger

insulation: materials used to prevent heat from escaping

irrigation: the addition of water to agricultural land using sprinklers, pumps, or pipes

livestock: domesticated animals raised for the production of meat or milk

maize: plant that produces sweet corn

medicinal: having the properties of a medicine

millet: cereal grown for its seeds or hay

monitor: see and record

nutrient: substance required by a living thing for growth and energy

organic: derived from living things such as plants and animals

organic matter: remains of dead plants and animals

organism: a living thing, such as an animal or plant, that is capable of reproduction and growth

ozone: a toxic gas that consists of three atoms of oxygen; a major source of pollution on the Earth

percolate: to drain or seep through

pesticide: any chemical compound that is used to kill pests

pollutant: substance that contaminates

predator: animal that kills and eats other animals

runoff: water that flows across the surface of the ground

salinity: amount of salt in a fluid

topsoil: upper layer of soil that is usually darker and richer than subsoil

toxic: containing poison

treat: to apply special substances to give a particular quality

urban: related to city or town

volatile organic compound: carbon-rich chemical that evaporates at room temperature

waste: unwanted material

wetland: water-covered area of land such as swamp or marsh

yield: an amount of a product produced on an area of land